Our Cam

MW01107539

By Stella Medina

Illustrated by Farida Zaman

Target Skill Setting

Scott Foresman
is an imprint of

We went to the campground.

I picked a nice spot for us.

It was at the big blue lake.

I pushed one rock.

Dad pushed more rocks to make a fire pit.

"Nice job, Dad!" I called.

Mom placed the tent here.

I helped Mom.

"Nice job, Mom," I said.

Mom fixed the poles.

I dug holes for the poles.

"Nice job!" called Dad.

We pulled the tent up.

It went up. It looked like a home!

Nice job, Mom, Dad, and Bev!

I looked in the tent.

It felt nice and snug.

I jumped in. Time for bed!

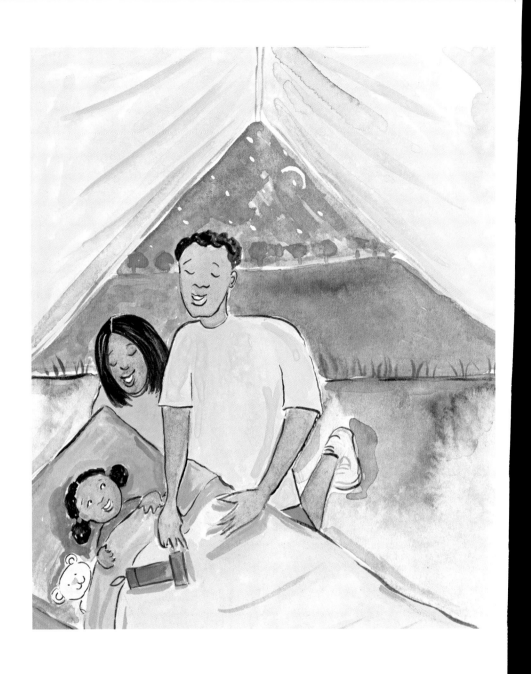

Mom and Dad tucked me in my bag.

I blinked and fell asleep.

Nice job, Mom and Dad and Bev!